Gentle Hands
and
Gentle Feet

Lisa Reynolds Amy

To order additional copies of this book, contact:
Xlibris
844-714-8691
www.Xlibris.com
Orders@Xlibris.com

ISBN: Softcover   979-8-3694-3842-8
       Hardcover   979-8-3694-3841-1
       EBook   979-8-3694-3843-5

Print information available on the last page

Rev. date: 01/31/2025

Gentle Hands
and
Gentle Feet

GENTLE HANDS

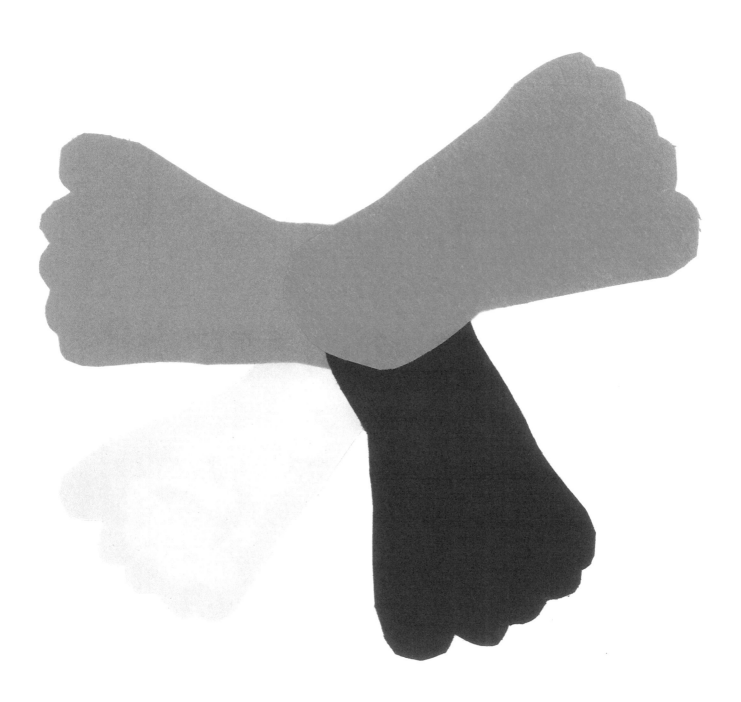

GENTLE FEET

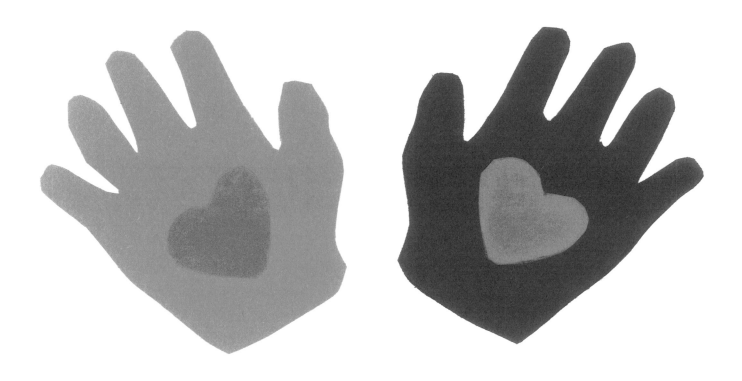

HELP US KEEP THE FRIENDS WE MEET

GENTLE HANDS
DON'T BALL
UP TIGHT

MAKING FISTS
TO PUNCH
OR FIGHT

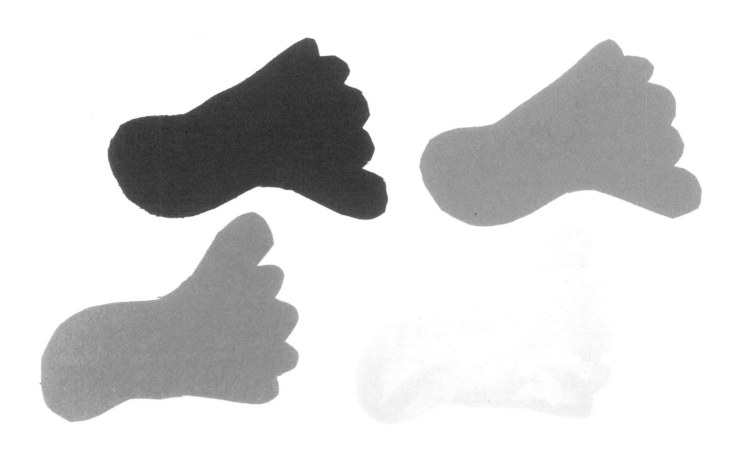

GENTLE FEET
WALK! NOT RUN!

UNLESS YOUR OUTSIDE HAVING FUN!

GENTLE HANDS AND GENTLE FEET!

HELP US KEEP THE FRIENDS WE MEET!